HALLOWEEN

Romantic Art

and Customs of Yesteryear

HALLOWEEN

Romantic Art and Customs of Yesteryear

Diane C. Arkins

PELICAN PUBLISHING COMPANY
Gretna 2000

ISBN 1-56554-712-8

Printed in Korea
Published by Pelican Publishing Company, Inc.
1000 Burmaster Street, Gretna, Louisiana 70053

Dedicated to my beloved canine companions past, present, and future

Vintage postcard marked series 216B. Mailed Springfield, Ohio, October 30, 1912.

CONTENTS

H. B. Griggs artist-signed postcard marked L.& E. series 2262. Mailed Illinois, October 28, 1910.

PROLOGUE

From my earliest adventures in the wonderland of trick-or-treating to a memorable first jack o'lantern, I've always harbored a special fondness for Halloween. For sentimentalists like myself, such potent happy memories rarely abandon the child who dwells within and, like many other accidental collectors, I came to develop an affection for the wonderful old-fashioned memorabilia whose images rekindled recollections of special Octobers gone by. Little did I realize when I casually acquired a few vintage Halloween postcards back in 1984 that my affection for these splendid little works of art—and for the holiday itself—would eventually lead to a book.

The colorful fortune-telling rituals and romantic customs described in this volume have been culled from a wide assortment of magazine stories and party planning guides published from 1900 to the 1930s. In repeating the old chants and poems, the traditional old-fashioned spelling of Hallowe'en has been preserved.

It should be noted that this mostly forgotten folklore is presented herein for the purpose of revisiting a unique part of America's past *only*, and modern sensibilities dictate that common sense and complete, utter dedication to safety concerns govern any attempts whatsoever to duplicate these traditions, and the old customs are most certainly not, repeat not, in any way intended for children.

It is my sincerest hope that you will enjoy this celebration of vintage Halloween postcards and other ephemera as you become acquainted with the spirited and beguiling romantic Halloween fortune-telling rituals of yesteryear.

DIANE C. ARKINS
OCTOBER 1999

Circa 1915 postcard. Postally unused.

HALLOWE'EN

Why are we gathered here? 'Tis the Hallowe'en.
Spookiest time of year, mystic Hallowe'en.
Strange things are all around,
Ghosts glide without a sound.
Everywhere spooks abound, on this mystic Hallowe'en.

Brownies their pranks will play on this Hallowe'en.
Goblins will prowl till day, this mystic Hallowe'en.
Elfins so gay and bright,
Frolic and dance all night.
Witches will cause you fright, on this mystic Hallowe'en.

Maidens their fate may tell on this Hallowe'en.
Of him they love so well learn on this Hallowe'en.
Learn what his trade may be,
If he'll be true to thee.
Maybe his face they'll see, this mystic Hallowe'en.
Haste then thy fate to learn on this mystic Hallowe'en.

Haste where candles burn, this mystic Hallowe'en.
Come, try thou every charm,
Bravely face each alarm.
Fair maid ne'er came to harm, on a mystic Hallowe'en.

The Complete Hallowe'en Book, *1915*

Halloween postcard marked No. 142. Mailed Toledo, Ohio, October 28, 1910.

INTRODUCTION

H. B. Griggs artist-signed postcard marked L.& E. series 2262. Postally unused.

"O, is my true love tall and grand?
O, is my sweetheart bonny?"

Am I fated to fall in love? . . . destined to marry? Does the one I love, love me best? Few things have delighted star-struck lovers more than a telling glimpse into the future, and throughout the ages, holidays associated with the essence of romance have offered opportunities to query Fate regarding matters of the heart. With its sweet sentiments, paper lace confections, and declarations of undying love, Valentine's Day has traditionally been the star on the romantic's calendar. Once upon an old-fashioned time, though, another much-celebrated occasion was highly regarded as an ideal time to peer into the future in terms of love and marriage, fate and fortune.

Welcome to the romantic side of Halloween!

Should it be surprising that a late autumn day customarily associated with eerily grinning jack-o'-lanterns, black cats yeow-ing in the moonlit haze, and mischievous parades of spirits that go "BOO!" in the night is also closely linked with sentiments of love, consider Halloween's rich history of romantic augury. From ancient times into the early decades of the twentieth century, this mystical occasion has been feted with quaint soothsaying rituals that bestowed fortune-telling properties on everything from the fruits of the harvest to household items as ordinary as mirrors, vessels of water, and balls of yarn.

Observed on the last night of October, Halloween is a colorful union of customs that evolved from the old Celtic festival days of Samhain, an annual observance of summer's end filled with mystic rites led by Druidic priests, and ancient Roman celebrations honoring Pomona, the goddess of fruits, seeds, and crops. When

the Christian church undertook to expand its influence, it attempted to undermine these established pagan influences by amalgamating the old rituals under the religious-oriented auspices of All Saint's, or Hallow's, Day. The night preceding this feast thus became known as All Hallow's Eve(n) or abbreviated in the old vernacular to Hallowe'en.

Circa 1924 Beistle Company, fairy placecard.

The age-old fortune-telling rituals that had developed under these sundry influences ultimately followed mid-nineteenth century Scottish, English, and Irish immigrants to their new homes in America, and by the turn of the twentieth century, the customs had taken root as popular Halloween party revels.

In the form of high-spirited seasonal balls, barn dances, masquerade parties, progressive dinners, and bridge socials, as well as church or club get-togethers, the typical early-twentieth-century Halloween event provided a properly chaperoned forum where hopeful romantics might steal a glance, share a dance, and coyly propel the progress of a relationship. The early 1900s were, after all, still an era when strict Victorian mores continued to dictate an exceptionally modest approach to interaction with members of the opposite sex. Real women dared not even converse with a man to whom they had not been formally introduced; "tactful" ladies would not suggest undertaking correspondence with a man, and it was considered essential that a girl of sixteen be chaperoned by a female relative during lengthy visits to the dentist.

S. Bergman No. 9076. Mailed Martin, Michigan, October 22, 1914.

"Don't let (any man) touch the tip of your little finger until he has the right," admonished one 1913 etiquette manual. "You'll be glad you didn't when the right man appears." In this atmosphere of commanding protocols, concerns over when, to whom, or even *if* one would marry were of such importance that romance-minded singles were highly receptive to the potential of playful fortune-telling rituals. Enter the old-fashioned Halloween party.

For inspiration on creating a hauntingly merry atmosphere for their Halloween events, organizers found ample advice in popular periodicals such as *Harper's Bazaar, The Ladies' Home Journal, The Delineator, The Modern Priscilla*, and *Woman's Home Companion*, as well as party planning guides like the highly-imaginative *Bogie Books*, published in the 1910s and 1920s by Dennison Manufacturing Company of Framingham, Massachusetts. These publications dished out clever inspiration for every detail from invitations, decorations, and party favors to refreshments and entertainment; they also made it clear that no gathering was complete without soothsaying games and revels.

"Telling fortunes is an indispensable feature of the Hallowe'en frolic," *The Ladies' Home Journal* told its readers in 1914. "No Hallowe'en party is complete unless many of the old-time games and stunts are tried," hostesses were reminded by Dennison's 1926 *Bogie* book. "Even if dancing is to supply the entertainment, an opportunity for 'Ducking for Apples,' 'Blowing Out Lighted Candles,' and 'Cutting the Flour Cake' should be included."

At the same time that these fanciful old-fashioned fortune-telling rituals were being embraced anew as party amusements, the nation was also smitten with the phenomenon of the illustrated picture postcard. These were not the polychrome Holiday Inn/Eiffel Tower/ "Wish You Were Here" variety of postcard so familiar to modern tourists, but rather enchanting little works of art resplendent with vibrant color, elegant embossing, and lively detail. Inexpensive to both buy and send, these eye-catching missives were used to impart news and glad tidings as routinely as we pick up the phone or send e-mail today. For the first two decades of the twentieth century, a period known to modern collectors as the "Golden Age of Postcards," illustrated cards were marketed for every imaginable holiday and reason. With its aura of mystery and vibrant images of will o' the wisps, glowing lanterns, and mischievous "bogeys" or elves, Halloween became a colorful standout in postcard imagery. Halloween postcards of this era, like the ones

Vintage Halloween postcard, circa 1915.

1924 "elf & pumpkin" folding fortune placecard made by The Beistle Company, Shippensburg, Pennsylvania. The pumpkin folds to stand on its own and the owl fortune tab can be raised and lowered.

that illustrate this book, are sought after by collectors and tell stories of harvest revels and flirtations with a touch of old-fashioned grace and romance that is impossible to resist.

The playfully nostalgic images of scrub-faced youngsters, whimsical "veggie people" characters, and alluring elegantly attired young women bear a stark contrast to the more realistically gruesome and genuinely horrifying depictions popular of late. These enchanting Halloween images of yesteryear bore a merrier air of mystery more likely to effect mild spells of teeth-chattering fright than any serious attacks of terror, and postcard motifs gaily depicted Halloween divinations or wished their recipients luck in those they undertook.

As generations passed, courting rituals became far less rigid. The playful post-Victorian matchmaking customs of Halloween gave way to (sub)urban sprawl and the more child-oriented door-to-door cavalcade of candy known as trick-or-treating. Aside from apple-bobbing, the old rituals were mostly forgotten. Despite their lengthy sabbatical, though, neither the vivid decorative imagery of Halloweens past nor the quaint soothsaying traditions of old have lost their charm. If anything, the

Circa 1910 postcard. Postally unused.

engaging rhymes and chants, trials and tests from this more genteel era seem more appealing than ever when viewed in the impersonal glare of a high-tech world.

The ancient rituals that featured the lively antics of burning nuts, mirrors that reflect a very special "face value," and a charm-filled old Irish potluck known as *caulcannon* might not have held the answers to every young single's wishes but, without a doubt, they surely offered our ancestors a winsome way to search. This volume will introduce you to many old tests and charms as it guides you in revisiting the old-fashioned spirit of the holiday.

And so carve your jack o'lanterns bold and bright, and deck the halls in festive fashion as you discover the unbridled merriment that attended this mystic day once upon an old-fashioned time.

Halloween postcard marked series 1239A. Postally unused.

H. B. Griggs artist-signed postcard No. 2214. Mailed Lindsey, Ohio, October 31, 1908.

PARTIES

Hallowe'en's the one time
Simply, purely fun time;
Full of superstitions
Born of old traditions;
Gnome and elf and fairy,
Witch and ghost make merry
On this last of dear October's days.

At the sinking sun time,
When the day is done time,
As the light grows dimmer,
Pranks begin to simmer.
And bewitching mystery,
Adds again to th' history
Of the last of dear October's days.

Charms are in the air
And spells are everywhere;
Airy visitations,
And hallucinations;
Matrimony, patron saint,
Weaves her superstitions quaint,
In this last of dear October's days.

Hallowe'en Happenings, *1921*

HALLOWEEN

Romantic Art
and Customs of Yesteryear

Halloween postcard marked No. 321.

FRUITS OF FANCY

Apple and Seeds

THE POWER OF THE LUCKY APPLE

If you have ducked for apples and have an apple won,
Your duties have not ended— indeed they've just begun.
That apple must be hidden, beneath your pillow white,
And then you'll see your sweetheart in your dreams that mystic night.
Another superstition tells a girl the fruit to eat,
As she combs her hair at midnight, if she would her true love meet.
He will gaze into her mirror where his image will be found,
But for fear that he will vanish, she must NEVER LOOK AROUND!

The Jolly Hallowe'en Book, *1937*

Which came first, the romantic's curious nature or the fortune-teller's clairvoyant powers? Puzzles like this can make inquirers' heads spin, but when it comes to old-fashioned Halloween fortune-telling rituals, one thing is clear: apples have played a prominent role from the very start.

The apple has been regarded a potent symbol of love and fertility dating back to the days of ancient Rome when harvest celebrations held around the first of November were dedicated to Pomona, the Goddess of Orchards, Seeds, and Crops and, over time, they have proven to be a soothsaying fruit of amazing versatility.

A HALLOWE'EN APPLE

We'll hang an apple and bite it by turns
And thus find an answer that everyone learns
Now, this is not magic, so don't feel alarm
For I have the answer and you have the charm.

Verse from old Halloween postcard

The popular party game of "Snap Apple" made a lively contribution to early-twentieth-century Halloween celebrations. A most basic version of this old English stunt required participants to use their teeth to capture an apple from amongst those gaily suspended from the ceiling by sturdy ribbons or string. The first to successfully perform this feat would be the first to marry.

E. C. Banks artist-signed postcard. Mailed Philadelphia, Pennsylvania, November 1, 1919.

"Mirror Series" postcard No. 248E, marked LSC. Postally unused.

Postcard marked B.W. 374, printed in Germany. Postally unused.

Harper's Bazaar described a more daring version of this fortune-telling stunt in 1907:

> "There was much merriment over the whirling stick. Upon one end of this an apple was impaled; upon the other stood a lighted candle. A string was attached near the apple, and the stick suspended from the ceiling, balanced so that it hung horizontally. It was then set whirling and players, hands still bound behind, were each given a few minutes' turn to try for a bite out of the apple's fat cheek. Around and around whirled the stick, so rapidly that the candle flame brushed noses and chins in the sauciest manner."

Anyone able to meet this substantial challenge was destined to find happiness involving affairs of the heart. Those who encountered the candle were, unsurprisingly, fated to experience misfortune . . . along with the possibility of singed eyebrows!

Halloween postcard, postmarked 1917.

THE SPELL OF THE APPLE PARING

Pare an apple, take the skin,
And fling it straight behind you;
Whatever letter it may frame,
That will begin your true love's name,
And (s)he will surely find you.

Bright Ideas for Hallowe'en, *1920*

THE APPLE PARINGS

With a sharp knife pare an apple
Round and round and round.
Toss the paring o'er your shoulder—
The initial found
Will be of the one you'll marry—
Do not be afraid!
'Tis an old prophetic omen
Good for man or maid.

The Jolly Hallowe'en Book, *1937*

Raphael Tuck & Sons "Hallowe'en" series of Post Cards, No. 174. Mailed Guthrie, Oklahoma, October 23, 1910.

E. C. Banks artist-signed postcard. Mailed Manchester, New Hampshire, year illegible.

In the mystic shadow of All Hallow's Eve, skillful apple paring could be employed to reveal clues about the identity of one's future mate. The lovelorn maiden who practiced this charm would pare her apple into a single continuous length and then toss the peeling over her shoulder. The shape in which it landed was believed to form her sweetheart's first initial. To strengthen such prophesies, fortune-seekers could repeat inspirational rhymes like this:

By this magic paring I wish to discover,
The first letter of the name of my true lover.
Three times round with movement slow,
Then upon the floor lie low;
Show me, if you know the same,
The letter of my true love's name.

Halloween postcard marked H15 CN. Mailed Brooklyn, New York, October 27, 1920.

Postcard marked B. W. 374, printed in Germany. Mailed Wilmington, Ohio, October 29, 1909.

If fate played a cruel trick and no letter could be identified from the peeling, it was interpreted as a sign that the inquirer would not marry. Thankfully, misfortune-telling of such a disappointing nature could slyly be side-stepped: "This trick positively cannot fail," was the advice endorsed on one turn-of-the-century postcard. "The peeling falls in such peculiar shapes, any bright girl can make out whatever initial she chooses."

WE'RE TELLING OUR FORTUNES

(an apple-paring song)

We're telling our fortunes,
Our secrets with you we share.
For charms work like magic on Hallowe'en night,
There's always a spell in the air.
Who shall it be?
How shall I know?
O'er the right shoulder our parings we throw.
Then his initial will come into sight,
O there's a charm in the Hallowe'en night,
A charm in the Hallowe'en night.

We're telling our fortunes,
Come join in the fun,
Now pick out your apple and see . . .
Just who you will wed e'er this old year is done,
And who your knight errant will be.
Who shall it be?
How shall we know?
O'er the right shoulder our parings we throw.
Then his initial will come into sight.
O there's a charm in the Hallowe'en night,
A charm in the Hallowe'en night.

Hallowe'en Frolic, *1908*

"Mirror Series" postcard No. 248A, marked LSC. Mailed Gloucester, Massachusetts, October 25, 1912.

One explanation regarding the origin of bobbing for apples traces the custom to the ancient Celtic belief that an enchanted Island of Apples might be reached by water's passage. In any case, revelers at Halloween parties of yesteryear eagerly responded to calls of "Hands behind your back! Use your teeth. Bob for your fortune underneath" and tried to snatch floating fruits bearing the names of their sweethearts.

The task was fraught with hurdles, as buoyant pippins dipped to evade capture. *The Delineator* magazine described the merry antics in its October 1894 issue:

> "The (gents) set to work 'bobbing' for the elusive red apples floating upon the water that filled the tub to the brim. The apples had a most exasperating faculty of slipping away at the merest touch, so that when one persistent young man succeeded in grasping an apple firmly between his teeth, he merited (his fortune)."

Halloween postcard mailed Westphalia, Indiana, October 30, 1909.

S. Bergman, New York, postcard. Mailed Center Strafford, New Hampshire, October 26, 1917.

German-made Halloween postcard marked No. 2243. Mailed Elgin, Illinois, October 30, 1911.

An apple caught on the very first attempt represented a true love that would be returned in kind. Those captured on subsequent tries represented fickleness or, ultimately, a sign from Fate to target a different suitor. The apple prizes could then either be placed beneath their captors' pillows—to inspire sweet dreams of a lover, naturally!—or cut open, their seeds counted to telling rhymes like these:

One seed, a journey,
Two seeds, a wealth.
Three seeds, true love,
Four seeds, health.
Five seeds, a quarrel.
Six seeds, fame.
Seven seeds, betrothal.
Eight, a new name.
Nine seeds, travel,
Ten seeds, a ring.
Eleven seeds a fortune,
To you will bring.

The Giant Hallowe'en Book, *1934*

Or,

One shows an enemy;
Two, a new friend;
Three, your luck is going to mend.
Four, a short sickness;
Five, some new clothes;
Six, a pleasant journey shows.
Seven, a lovers' quarrel;
Eight says twice you'll wed;
Nine, a long life before you're dead.
Ten, you'll be happy;
Eleven, riches galore;
Twelve says of children you'll have four.
Thirteen brings honor;
Fourteen, a good name;
Fifteen brings you political fame.

Hallowe'en Merrymakers, *1930*

American Colorgravure Post Card Hallowe'en series 182, subject 2761. Mailed Holyoke, Massachusetts, October 27, 1910.

Alternatively, the seeds from an apple could be placed on the palm of one hand and the number remaining after the hands were clapped together could be interpreted as follows:

One I love,
Two I love,
Three I love, I say;
Four I love with all my heart;
Five I cast away.
Six he loves,
Seven she loves,
Eight they both love;
Nine he comes,
Ten he tarries,
Eleven he courts and
Twelve he marries.
Thirteen, they quarrel; fourteen they part;
Fifteen, they die with a broken heart.
Sixteen, wishes; seventeen, riches;
All the rest are little witches (children).

Spooky Hallowe'en Entertainments, *1923*

Or, several seeds could be designated to represent different suitors and then placed upon forehead, eyelids, or cheeks. The seed that remained in place the longest was said to signal the identity of the future mate. Those familiar with this augury, however, knew that fate might be "influenced" with a sly wriggle of the nose.

The bounty of novel apple-related divinations did not end here by any means, and when the night was ripe with mystery and magic, intrepid romantics were advised to coax the fates with rituals like these:

• Eat an apple in front of a mirror on Halloween and an image of your true love will appear in the mirror to ask for the last bite.

Halloween postcard marked No. 247. Mailed Bayonne, New Jersey, October 31, 1910.

• Cut open an apple on Halloween night and learn your fortune by this rhyme:

One seed shows you'll get a letter,
Two a dish you're going to break.
Three seeds, you'll hear some good news,
Four, a ride you soon will take.
Five, you will be disappointed,
Six, you're going to meet a friend.
Seven brings you a surprise,
Eight, some money you will spend.
Nine shows there's pleasure coming,
Ten, you'll have something to wear.
Eleven, you will take a trip,
Twelve, some good luck you will share.
Thirteen seeds, you'll have a fright,
Fourteen, your future days are bright.

Kiddies' Hallowe'en Book, *1931*

• Slice an apple in half and examine the seeds within. If only two are round, they portend an early marriage. Three signal a legacy; four, great wealth; five, a sea voyage; six, great fame as an orator or singer; seven, possession of an item most desired.

Halloween postcard marked No. 142. Mailed Boston, Massachusetts, October 24, 1911.

COUNTING THE APPLE SEEDS

The wind was east—fast fell the snow;
We said; "'Tis a stormy night,"
And crowded to the hearth-fire's glow
That shone so warm and bright;
With rosy fruit each hand was filled
From the home orchard near,
When suddenly the laugh was still,—
"We'll count the seeds," I hear.

'Tis one, "he loves"—that's Nettie Day;
"Two," "three," he loves the same,
For Willie "five," he casts away;
Rob's "four" his heart will claim;
Then "six, he loves," and "seven, loves she;"
Ah! "both love!" now shouts Jim
As he the lucky "eight" can see,
An omen good for him.

Then "nine, he comes," the door bell rings,
And Doris sets a chair
For one whose coming welcome brings,
Who joins the revel there;
Ah! "ten, he tarries,"—Jeanie's lot,
But in her heart she knows
The one she named has ne'er forgot,
However fortune goes.

"Eleven, he courts,"—the apple's heart
Alone, fair Edith knows,
For Phil, beside her, gives a start,
And lacks his calm repose,
For "twelve he marries" fair and straight
His apple's seeds they view;
He whispers, "I believe in fate,
Dear, if that fate be you."

Annie L. Jack, Good Housekeeping,
January 8, 1887

• Take two apple seeds and designate one "riches," the other "poverty." Stick them on your eyelids; the one that remains there longest foretells your fate.

• Cut open an apple. Put its seeds between your hands and clap once. Count those remaining afterward to reveal your fate:

One I love,
Two I love,
Three I love, I say;
Four I love with all my heart;
Five I cast away.
Six he loves,
Seven she loves,
Eight he comes to woo.
Nine he tarries,
Ten he marries,
And that's my fortune true.

Hallowe'en Happenings, *1921*

Halloween postcard marked L. & E. No. 7027, printed in Germany. Postally unused.

• Count the seeds of an apple to this rhyme to learn the vocation of your future mate:

Girls:
Rich man, poor man, beggar-man, thief;
Doctor, lawyer, merchant, chief.

Boys:
Rich girl, poor girl, pretty girl, brunette;
Sweet girl, neat girl, lazy girl, coquette.

The last seed decides your fate.

• Place three apple seeds pointing toward you, side by side, on a hot stove. Name one seed Toil, another Ease, the third Travel. The one that remains closest to you after the heat makes them jump reveals your lot in life.

• Halve an apple and match the number of seeds it contains with these fortunes:

One, a letter shall appear,
Two, you'll meet a friend who's dear;
Three, you're going to be miffed,
Four, you'll soon receive a gift.
Five, you'll have a glad surprise,
Six, something lost will meet your eyes;
Seven brings you a holiday,
Eight brings company from away;
Nine, you take a trip somewhere,
Ten, you'll have a love affair.
Eleven, you will quarrel and part,
Twelve, you'll for the altar start.
Thirteen brings you joy and health,
Fourteen brings a bag of wealth.

Spooky Hallowe'en Entertainments, *1923*

Halloween postcard marked F. A. Owen Co., Dansville, New York. Postally unused.

PROPHESIES OF "NUTCRACK NIGHT"

Most people are aware of the potential for "good things" to come in small packages, and once upon an old-fashioned Halloween some of the most potent and popular prognosticators assumed the Lilliputian stature of nuts.

Easily the augural equivalent of apples, nuts were also abundant at harvest time and their perceived ability to provide guidance pertaining to matters of the heart was so highly respected in the north of England that people there have long referred to Halloween as "Nutcrack Night."

One traditional divination associated with walnuts called upon fortune-seekers to circle a nut tree at midnight on Halloween while repeating the phrase "Let (s)he that is my true love bring me some walnuts." In doing so, they would be treated to a fleeting vision of their future mates gathering nuts nearby.

A merry launching of "walnut boats" afforded an offbeat way of divining fortunes. First, diminutive "boats" were crafted by removing the meats from walnut shells and then using melted wax to secure a different color candle in each half. The candles were designated to represent individual partygoers and then lit as the quaint vessels were set afloat in a large tub of water. The courses they took were observed to determine the fate of their nominees.

Halloween postcard marked "12," copyright by Florence Bamberger. Postally unused.

A pair of shells that glided together side-by-side represented owners who would share a similar destiny; if they glided apart, so would their relationship. If a man and a woman's boats came together, the two were destined to wed. The first shell to reach the opposite side of the tub represented the one who'd first reach the "port of matrimony" while the person whose candle was extinguished first was fated to be a bachelor or spinster.

The designated "captains" of tiny crafts that huddled together would remain close, while solitary, stranded vessels symbolized the fate of an outcast or loner; the candle to remain lit longest identified the person who would live longest in the assembled group; and a shell that sank was said to foreshadow death. Fortunately, the impact of this final ghastly prediction might be diminished by assurances that the prediction of "death" actually symbolized the demise of hopes or aspirations.

If (s)he loves me, pop and fly;
If (s)he hates me, lie and die.

The lion's share of auguries associated with nuts focused on interpreting their actions as they roasted in the flames of bonfire or hearth. In general, nuts that blazed brightly foretold prosperity, while those that smoldered or turned dark signaled misfortune. It was, however, those charms by which walnuts and chestnuts were deigned to represent individuals and their vigor in the fire observed that the most romantic fortunes were told. Here's how the tests of Nutcrack Night could be coaxed to reveal their secrets:

• Designate a pair of hazelnuts to represent two different sweethearts and toss the nuts into an open flame.

Halloween postcard marked B37. Postally unused.

Should a nut burst, that lover will prove unfaithful; a nut that burns instead with a steady glow until it turns to ashes denotes a lover who will be loving and true. If both nuts burn steadily, the inquirer's heart will be torn between the two.

• Use a pair of chestnuts to determine what course a romance might take. Two nuts that burn quietly side-by-side in the fire presage a contented union. Should one nut suddenly explode, the relationship is doomed to be short-lived or marked by quarrels, strife, and separations.

These glowing nuts are emblems true
Of what in human life we view;
The ill-matched couple fret and fume,
And thus in strife themselves consume;
Or from each other wildly start,
And with a noise forever part.
But see the happy, happy pair,
Of genuine love and truth sincere;
With mutual fondness while they burn,
Still to each other kindly turn;
And as vital sparks decay,
Together gently sink away;
Till life's fierce trials being past,
Their mingled ashes rest at last.

Games For Hallowe'en, *1912*

Circa 1912 Halloween postcard. Postally unused.

• Designate nuts to represent love interests and observe their behavior in the fire. A nut that burns steadily symbolizes a faithful, gentlemanly mate; one that crackles or pops represents an untrustworthy spouse whose wife will be kept "hopping" to keep him in tow.

• Place a pair of chestnuts named for yourself and a lover in an open fire. If the nuts burn quietly, a peaceful married life can be expected; if they sputter and crackle, the marriage will be marked by quarrels. Nuts that remain apart signal divorce or separation. Those that burn black foretell a life of solitude and poverty; those that blaze up, on the other hand, foreshadow great prosperity.

• Test the faithfulness of two sweethearts by placing three nuts, one also to represent yourself, on the grate. A nut that jumps away represents a love that will be unfaithful. The destiny of the nuts that remain together can be foretold by the way they burn: bright flames are indicative of passionate love and happiness while slow, smoky burning foreshadows unhappiness and fleeting affection.

Halloween postcard marked H13 CN. Mailed Louisville, Kentucky, October 30, 1923.

Ellen Clapsaddle artist-signed card for International Art Publ. Co., New York, Berlin. Mailed Peoria, Illinois, October 30, 1911.

CHESTNUTS ON THE COALS

These glowing nuts are emblems true
Of what the future holds for you;
The one which soon doth hiss and fume,
To fret and scold will oft presume;
If with hisses both are rife—
Ah me! You'll lead a stormy life;
If from each other they wildly start
Then fate foretells that you shall part;
But if they burn with quiet glow,
A life of joy and peace you'll know.

Hallowe'en Fun, *1927*

• Designate two nuts to represent a man and a woman. Place the nuts in the fire as close together as possible and observe the manner in which they burn. If "he" leaps from the flames, it is a sign that he will desert her; if "she" leaps forth, she will be the unfaithful one. To be indicative of a happy relationship, the nuts will burn uneventfully side by side.

H. B. Griggs artist-signed postcard, L. & E. series 2272. Dated October 30, 1914.

TRIAL BY FIRE

Name two nuts for man and maid
Put them in the fire.
If they burn in peaceful way
True love will transpire.
If they pop and fly apart,
Trouble will ensue;
Separation will come fast,
They're ill fated too.

The Jolly Hallowe'en Book, *1937*

• Name three chestnuts for yourself and two sweethearts and put them in the fire. If the nuts separate, so will those for whom they are named. Those jumping toward the fire will move to a warmer climate; those jumping away from the fire, to a colder climate. Two gentlemen jumping toward one another signifies rivalry.

Two hazel-nuts I threw into the flame,
And to each nut I gave a sweetheart's name;
This with the loudest bounce me sore amazed,
That in a flame of brightest color blazed;
As blazed the nut, so may thy passion grow,
For 'twas thy nut that did so brightly glow.

Curiosities of Popular Customs, *1897*

Postcard marked series No. 7146. Mailed Iowa, October 25, 1913.

Circa 1920s heavy cardboard die-cut anthropomorphic carrot decoration by Dennison Manufacturing, measures 1¾ x 4½.

IN THE HARVEST GARDEN

When the moon of Hallowe'en
Is sailing full and high
I wish good luck to follow
All the merry tricks you try.

Verse from old Halloween postcard

By the grace of God in nature, well and truly anything that sprouts from the earth is imbued with a magic of sorts. For early twentieth-century romantics, though, the harvest garden was especially ripe with fortune-telling symbolism. An old English custom known as "scadding the peas" called for a lone bean to be placed in one amongst many pea pods. When the boiled peas were served, the diner who discovered the bean was assured of good fortune.

In a custom that might seem more common sense than magic, it was believed that fortune-seekers who hid in cornfields on Halloween would overhear what would transpire in the coming year. Dreams of one's future spouse were said to come to those who gathered milfoil, or yarrow, on Halloween and slept with it under their pillows.

Of all the mystical properties found in the bounty of the harvest garden, the most unlikely horticultural crystal ball may well have been the homely "kailstock" or kale plant. This openly leafy cabbage and kissin' cousin to broccoli and kohlrabi was such a venerable nineteenth-century garden staple that farmers of yesteryear tended some twenty-six different varieties. Notable amongst them was a cattle feed crop known as "tree cabbage" that could grow to heights of nine feet and whose stem could be made into a novel walking stick.

Circa 1920s embossed die-cut anthropomorphic cabbage head on crepe paper hat.

It was, however, the less showy varieties of kale that were sought out by Halloween revelers keen to learn more about their future mates. Mimicking an ancient Scottish tradition known as "pou (pull) the stalks," intrepid romantics walked hand-in-hand to the vegetable patch at night and, eyes tightly shut, picked the very first cabbage they encountered. The first fortune was offered in the harvesting: the ease or difficulty by which the root was released from the earth foretold the degree of effort required to win one's sweetheart.

Plants could then be assessed against this telling barometer of attributes: a full, green head symbolized an attractive young mate; a closed white stalk was indicative of an elderly or stingy spouse; dirt clinging to the plant's roots presaged wealth; clean roots foretold poverty; the flavor of the root—sharp, sweet, bitter, or insipid—was said to mimic the mate's disposition, while its shape—stout or lanky, bold or graceful—was taken to represent the mate's physical build.

A lad and lassie, hand in hand,
Each pull a stock of kail;
And like the stock, is future wife
Or husband, without fail.
If stock is straight, then so is wife,
If crooked, so is she;
If earth is clinging to the stock,
The puller rich will be.
And like the taste of each stem's heart,
The heart of groom or bride;
So shut your eyes, and pull the stocks,
And let the fates decide.

Bright Ideas for Hallowe'en, *1920*

Top: *Halloween postcard series 2471, printed in Germany. Mailed Derry, Pennsylvania, October 29, 1912.*

Right: *Ellen Clapsaddle artist-signed card for International Art Publ. Co., New York, Berlin. Mailed Grand Rapids, Michigan, year illegible.*

Circa 1912 Halloween postcard. Postally unused.

Following these tests, gentleman guests were asked to leave the room while the ladies' stalks were hung above the doorway and assigned numbers. As the men returned, the initial of the first to reenter was deemed to represent that of the future mate of the maiden whose stalk was number one. The second entrant's name was symbolic of the initial of the husband-to-be for the owner of stalk number two, and so on down the line. Alternatively, the kale could be taken home and placed behind the front door; the initial of its owner's future spouse would match that of the first man outside the family to enter therein.

An old Irish custom called for randomly harvested cabbage stalks to be named for partygoers. Clean, light-colored plants presaged entrance to Heaven; a cabbage darkened by frost signaled that its designee was headed for a substantially warmer and less desirable afterlife.

Elsewhere in the garden, Halloween revelers could tap a well of imaginative divinations like these:

- Take two long-stemmed roses and name one for yourself, the other for your true love. Without speaking to anyone, go to your room, kneel beside the bed, and twist the flower stems together. Gaze intently at your lover's rose as you repeat this rhyme:

> *Twine, twine, and intertwine,*
> *Let my love be wholly thine.*
> *If his heart be kind and true,*
> *Deeper grow his rose's hue.*

If your sweetheart is faithful, the color of his rose will appear to have darkened.

- Mix a handful of peas in a large pot of beans. Whilst glancing away, stir the pot and then lift a spoonful. A pea discovered amongst the beans denotes good luck for its finder during the coming twelve months. An alternate version of this augury holds that anyone who finds a pea will marry within a year.

German-made postcard dated October 31, 1911.

• Harvest oats the garden and learn your fate by this rhyme:

> *A maiden pulls three stalks of oats,*
> *And if, upon the third,*
> *That maiden finds no head of grain,*
> *Her marriage is assured.*
>
> Bright Ideas for Hallowe'en, *1920*

• Randomly carve the letters of the alphabet on the surface of a splendid specimen of pumpkin. Guide blindfold fortune-seekers to this harvest oracle where they can learn their true love's initials by pointing at the pumpkin with a hat pin or wand.

Pumpkins like this one, carved with letters of the alphabet, were used to help determine the initials of one's future mate.

• Go to the garden on Halloween and sow seeds of hemp while repeating this rhyme:

Hemp-seed, I saw thee,
Hemp-seed, I saw thee;
And (s)he that is to be my true love,
Come after me and draw thee.

Look over your left shoulder and a vision of your intended will appear.

• Dip a spoonful of corn kernels or beans and count them to the appropriate rhyme-the last from the spoon signals the occupation of your future mate.

For girls

Rich man, poor man,
Policeman, plumber,
Merchant, lawyer,
Doctor, drummer,
Blacksmith, grocer,
Druggist, teacher,
Artist, dentist,
Banker, preacher.

For boys

Rich girl, poor girl, suffragette,
Waitress, milliner, farmerette;
Schoolma'am, actress, stenographer,
Musician, trained nurse, dressmaker;
Bookkeeper, house maid, author, clerk,
Telephone girl and a lazy shirk.

Spooky Hallowe'en Entertainments, *1923*

• Name two peas for lovers and place them on a hot shovel. A pea that jumps symbolizes a lover who will prove unfaithful. If a pea ignites or burns, the one for whom it is named will be beloved.

Go to the garden where the beet patch grows full
On Hallowe'en night and begin to pull
At the stroke of twelve if a beet is straggly, sad lot for thee,
But if smooth and round, a happy life thine will be.

Verse from old Halloween postcard

Embossed cardboard die-cut cat musician approximately 9" tall, marked H.E. Luhrs.

Raphael Tuck and Sons "Hallowe'en" Post Cards series No. 183. Printed in Saxony. Postally unused.

The Ladies' Home Journal for October, 1919 63

The New Halloween Frolics

By Elizabeth Bissell

FOR a wall decoration on a stairway black crêpe paper honeycombed over orange looks well and is easy to do. The tops of the newel posts are rounded by pieces of wire, and an owl is set in the midst of a lotus flower. The "witch in the woods" would make a fine background for a twin-witch fortune teller seated in the foreground.

STARTLINGLY stunning, but graceful withal, is the doorway decoration. The pumpkin heads should all be the same size; the perspective of the photograph makes them appear here in assorted sizes. At the side of the doorway stack corn shocks or bunches of tall grass.

THIS mask is in place all the evening, when suddenly a girl wearing an orange-paper fringed skirt walks back of it, slips her head into the mask, ties the cape around her neck, and then steps through the fringed curtain into the room, leaving the doorway curtain intact. This new "stunt" makes a lot of fun. She may then serve "witches' brew" (fruit punch) from the kettle.

FOR the decoration of the table a Japanese umbrella is used as a foundation for the hanging centerpiece. The funny-faced lanterns are glass fish globes, and tiny red or blue light bulbs could be dropped into them. The place-card people have fortunes fastened to their backs.

WOULD you think that a huge cat's head could be made by simply opening a big black umbrella and pasting eyes, nose, mouth, ears and whiskers upon it? Just look at the fireplace and see.

AS PICTURESQUE as pretty is this window decoration. The details are from a new crêpe-paper design recently put on the market. Placed in a room with French doors decorated as in the lower left-hand picture on this page, one begins to feel the real Halloween atmosphere that lends itself to frolicking.

ON THE left a cardboard ghost is fastened to the inside of the door with pin tacks. Then the door is shut. The one in the party who can best take a joke and stand a shock is sent on some pretense to open the door, when the ghost confronts him. This original stunt has been tried out and was most successfully funny.

THE ghost is a talking machine "all dressed up" with sheets. A ghost-story record produces a realistic effect, especially in a darkened room. Children will be delighted with record stories suitable to their years.

This page from the October 1919 issue of The Ladies' Home Journal *illustrated a fabulous assortment of Halloween party decorating ideas.*

DECK THE HALLOWEEN HALLS

Hallowe'en parties are quite the style,
Please come to ours, prepared to smile,
As we ward off ill luck and evils and harms
With divers[e] old-fashioned fates and charms.

Hallowe'en Fun, *1927*

Festive yet frightful. Mellow but merry. Few celebrations have been as dependent upon mood and setting as Halloween parties and in the 1910s and 1920s, ambitious hostesses turned to popular magazines like *The Ladies' Home Journal*, *Woman's Home Companion*, *American Home*, *The Delineator*, *Harper's Bazaar*, *The Housekeeper*, and *The Modern Priscilla* for inspiration on outfitting the home or banquet hall in an atmosphere conducive to a scintillating evening of fortune-telling frolics.

The periodicals skillfully addressed every party detail from invitations (a turn-of-the-century issue of *Harper's Bazaar* suggested ringing invitees' doorbells and anonymously leaving invitations on their porches, along with small lighted jack o'lanterns) to refreshments (more than one magazine served up a wordplay menu of "sandwitches," deviled eggs, and devil's food cake). If chairs draped languidly with white sheets to resemble ghosts were a good idea, then grotesquely carved jack o'lanterns grimacing from every corner were mandatory.

"Bogie book" Halloween party guides were booklets published by Dennison Manufacturing Company of Framingham, Massachusetts, from the early 1900s through the 1920s, to show consumers imaginative ways of decorating with the company's paper products. This page from the 1913 edition shows a spooky mantel and fireplace decoration.

Every bit as imaginative as the suggestions themselves was the quaintly elegant prose early-twentieth-century wordsmiths employed to present them. Party scenes and decorating ideas were often so vividly established in the mind's eye that they seem to have turned the cliché tables and created some unique situations in which a few splendid words were worth a thousand pictures.

The delightful old prose is well worth revisiting here for contemporary readers to experience and savor the bewitching atmosphere in which the old soothsaying revels were practiced, and love might be won or lost at the blink of a magical eye.

The large hospitable house, usually brilliantly lighted, looked very dark, almost gloomy, as we neared it on the appointed evening. The broad front porch was lighted only by a very big Jack-o'-lantern with a placard directing us to "pull the bell and wait."

The way into the house was made very devious and winding. The stairs were trimmed with corn-stalks set closely, ears of corn, bright autumn leaves, and red berries of the black alder and bunches of small scarlet rose hips, the last being especially pretty and more graceful than stiff twigs of alder. Here and there were branches of white "wax or snow berries" from the old-fashioned shrub rarely found now except in very old gardens. An immense Jack-o'-lantern sat grinning benevolently from the newel-post.

The whole house was strikingly decorated with the autumnal spoils of the fields and woods. The bright golden brown of the fresh corn-stalks, which were used lavishly, combined with huge bunches of yellow and red ears of corn gave a true October air and color to the scene. In every available point jack-o'-lanterns, big or small, were placed. They scowled savagely or smiled jovially, as the carver had decreed, from many an otherwise dark corner, for the regular lights of the house were turned low.

"A Novel Hallowe'en Party,"
Harper's Bazaar, November 1904

Right, lead-in: *Embossed cardboard decorative cat face by H. E. Luhrs.*

1920 "Johnny Pumpkin Head" cardboard stand-up character by The Beistle Company, Shippensburg, Pennsylvania.

The very elements conspired to make the night one suggestive of witches' revels and uncanny spells. The rushing, shrieking wind drove the rain in blinding sheets, out of the tumult of which it was a two-fold joy to be ushered into fairy-land—a fairy-land evolved from corn, pumpkins, apples, candles and mirrors in happy combination. There were mirrors everywhere, big mirrors, medium-sized mirrors, and little, wee mirrors, all reflecting and multiplying countless candles that burned in candlesticks of every description, the most novel of which were those made from long-necked gourds, tiny squashes, oranges and very large pumpkins.

Across the top and down the sides of each doorway were hung festoons of yellow and white corn, the husks turned back to show the firm, glistening kernels. Each window was garlanded in like manner, as were the tops of mantels and picture-frames. Clusters of red ears, in all the brilliancy of artificial coloring, descended from chandeliers.

Here and there, in the most unexpected corners, Jack-o'-lanterns smiled or gnashed their teeth amid great shocks of corn or leered from lofty coigns of vantage. Queer little rotund Jacks, made from cucumber shells, grimaced in grotesque abandon from one mantelshelf, guarded by two solemn owls, fierce-eyed but stuffed!

The great hall and stairway were draped with fish-nets, through the meshes of which were thrust many ears of corn. A stately Jack at the newel-post, pointed dramatically up the stairs, where two other individuals of the same ilk posed as ushers.

"Merry Hallowe'en Larks,"
The Ladies' Home Journal, October 1903.

Left, lead-in: *Embossed cardboard decorative cat face by H. E. Luhrs.*

A page from the 1920 edition of the Dennison "Bogie Book" shows a delightful assortment of ideas for Halloween costumes made from crepe paper.

The Bogie Book.

Costumes for Hallowe'en Affairs

THE dress on the left has an underskirt of Orange Crepe No. 64, a plain waist and a flaring skirt of Black and White Stripe Crepe No. B&W1. A wire hoop pasted around the edge of the overskirt causes it to stand out. The hat is made by gathering a straight piece of crepe along one edge until it fits the head, and pasting a wire around the other edge. Fasten the gathered edge to a band and trim it with the striped crepe.

Child's dress with skirt and sleeves of Orange Crepe No. 65 and overdress of Orange and Black Tile Pattern No. 309. The bat is Cut-out No. H72.

The two-ruffle skirt of Orange Crepe No. 64 is cut in scallops and trimmed with cats' heads cut from Decorated Crepe No. H833. The three-scalloped cat crown is made of orange mat stock, and is held on by a band which fits the head.

The man's regalia slips on over the head. The orange portion is the full width of crepe. Pieces of black crepe pasted on front, back and at the sides give it a flare. The hat is a square of black mat stock pasted to a band.

Page twenty-five

The table of the ghosts is covered with black percaline, with a border of black bats against orange moons. A mirror plateau covered with autumn leaves occupies the center of the tables. From it rises a tall, thick, yellow candle around which white cardboard ghosts dance weirdly. Different-sized tissue-paper disks in all the autumn colorings—red, green, yellow, russet, orange—are arranged around the centerpiece and on some of them are placed silver dishes filled with bonbons, nuts, olives, etc. The place cards are yellow paper scrolls held by ghosts of smaller size.

"Hallowe'en Fun,"
The Ladies' Home Journal, October 1916

Of course there was a witch's hut, made by putting a screen across one corner of the room and hiding it with tall cornstalks. An old-fashioned lantern hung over the door, and the witch who lived here revealed the future of any who entered during the evening.

In decorating the laundry (room), ironing-boards were used to cover the sink and all but one of the set tubs, which was left open and filled with water. Rosy apples floated here in a border of leaves . . . Cornstalks, fastened here and there about the room, gave a cozy effect, and pumpkin jack-o-'lanterns grinned or scowled from every corner. Paper ears on some, and fringe of black tissue paper for hair and a hat stuck jauntily on another, made them look like witch's heads peering hideously out of the gloom. Fancy crepe paper was stretched above the tubs and black cats, witches, owls, and bats were pasted all over the walls. A pastel drawing of a witch hung over the stove.

"A Hallowe'en Masquerade,"
The Modern Priscilla, October 1912

"Before" and "After (the guests have arrived)." Halloween party decorating ideas presented in the October 1912 issue of The Modern Priscilla *magazine.*

A particularly pretty table fancy was shown at an informal evening party where the supper served was *en buffet*. Lighted jack-o'-lanterns were placed on the sideboard and a large weirdly-shaped Japanese lantern hung from the chandelier directly over the dining room table, which, however, had no lights upon it.

For a centerpiece, a dish or bowl of highly polished fruits looks most dainty, draped with an airy clematis. If for Hallowe'en a bare branch can rise from the center of the fruits on which can be perched two or three saucy looking paper owls.

Strings of small red apples and gilded nuts can descend from the chandelier, while loops of popcorn rubbed with phosphorus are effective when the only light is shed from jack o'lanterns.

Little crook-neck squashes, hollowed out, make delightful little horns of plenty to fill with bonbons or candied fruits, while apples and oddly shaped potatoes will serve nicely for candlesticks, having the candles colored red, green or yellow."

"Entertaining Our Friends,"
The Housekeeper, October 1909

These fanciful fortune-backed Halloween cat decorations for desserts were made of durable cardboard by Dennison Manufacturing Co. and packaged in a box of 12 that sold for 25 cents in 1924. A sample fortune: "Meeting many, liking few; always searching for someone new. Searching for a perfect mate—Make haste! Or you will be too late."

Postcard marked JED series 57B. Mailed Detroit, Michigan, October 28, 1917.

SWEET DREAMS

Turn your boots toward the street,
Leave your garters on your feet,
Put your stockings on your head—
You'll dream of the one you're going to wed.
Spooky Hallowe'en Entertainments, *1923*

Since the days when the ancient Celtic peoples observed Samhain, a summer's-end feast when spirits of the dead, both good and evil, were said to walk the earth, Halloween has been regarded as a mystic occasion when the ethereal separation between the living and spirit worlds was most easily penetrated. In an atmosphere so conducive to things supernatural, it's little wonder that the reveries of slumber were deemed to possess their own unique insights into the future.

One augury of yesteryear advised young maidens to rub the four posts of their bed with two pieces of lemon. If the man they loved felt in kind, he would appear in their dreams to present them with a pair of lemons. To coax visions of their future wives, young men were advised to dip their shirt-sleeves in the water of a south-running spring (one where three properties met no less!) and then go to bed in sight of the fire before which they had hung the shirts to dry. Sometime near midnight, spirits resembling their future wives would appear to turn the sleeves of the shirts so the opposite sides might dry.

Circa 1915 Halloween postcard. Postally unused.

Raphael Tuck & Sons "Hallowe'en" Post Cards series, No. 150. Postally unused.

Circa 1915 Halloween postcard. Postally unused.

At Halloween, sweet dreams for lovelorn ladies and gents were made of such rituals . . . and dreamy of fortunes like these:

• Place a glass of water containing a sliver of wood on your nightstand and repeat this rhyme before going to bed on Halloween night: "Husband mine that is to be, come this night and rescue me." During the night you will dream of falling from a bridge into a river, and of being rescued by your future mate, whose image will be crystal clear.

• Write the names of three sweethearts on slips of paper and put them beneath your pillow. If you dream of one of those named, you can be assured that person cares for you. If his is the name you draw out first in the morning, he will be the one you marry.

• Before going to sleep on Halloween night, designate different bedposts to represent music, art, literature, and business. The first bedpost you see upon awakening denotes your future vocation.

• Walk out the front door backward at the stroke of twelve on Halloween night and pick three blades of grass. Wrap the grass in orange paper and put it beneath your pillow to ensure that the evening's dreams will come true.

Valentine & Sons Publishing Co. Ltd., New York. Postally unused.

SOMEONE'S IN THE KITCHEN . . .

Gingerbread men could be eaten on Halloween night to ensure finding a real live mate.

Be sure that you make no mistake
But win the prize in the Hallowe'en cake.

Verse on old Halloween postcard

A century ago, Halloween revelers didn't need to look beyond the kitchen pantry for omens of what the future might hold. In English villages, for example, young ladies were known to succumb to the sweet ritual of eating gingerbread men on All Hallow's Eve under the belief that it would guarantee finding a mate in real life.

In Ireland, tiny fortune-telling tokens were baked into Halloween cakes or served up in a caulcannon (also called "calcannon" or "callcannon"), a traditional stew comprised of potatoes, parsnips, and onions. It was believed that the diner finding a coin in his serving would soon be the recipient of wealth. A tiny ring foretold marriage; a thimble, spinsterhood; a doll figure, children; and a button, mixed fortune.

Quite a different challenge awaited those who sought to peer into the future by way of the ancient Scottish custom known as the "Dumb Cake." By this charm, partygoers were required to maintain absolute silence as they kneaded small pieces of stiff dough with their left thumbs for fifteen minutes. Anyone who disturbed the quiet or touched the dough with the right thumb or fingers was fated to misfortune. Those who were able to resist speaking and handle the dough as directed could expect the fates to be benevolent and kind. As simple as it might seem, the task of keeping quiet amidst a group of merry Halloween revelers could pose a considerable challenge.

Valentine & Sons Publishing Co. Ltd., New York. Postally unused.

Postcard marked B.W. 374, printed in Germany. Mailed Philadelphia, Pennsylvania, October 30, 1909.

A different variation of the "Dumb Cake" ritual called for inquisitive romantics to take a piece of dough that had been prepared with water (but not spring water) and knead it in silence using their left thumbs. After the dough was shaped into small cakes, a new pin was used to etch the top of each with its maker's initials and those of her true love. At midnight the cakes were baked, and couples whose initials were still plainly visible afterward were destined to marry before the year was out.

THE CAKE OF SILENCE

The mystic cake of Hallowe'en
By seven maids is stirred,
They mix stiff dough of watered flour
But not one word is heard.
If any speaks, she is disgraced—
The last she'll be to wed.
She'll find no prince nor Lochinvar,
Just some poor stick instead.
When in the pan the dough is placed,
Each maid takes a new pin;
And pricks the initials of her own
And of her sweetheart in.
For just ten minutes then it bakes,
With silence still about,
Then those whose letters are still plain
Will wed e'er year is out.

The Jolly Hallowe'en Book, *1937*

Hearth and home played host to many other whimsical superstitions. "When will I marry?" "Does the one I love, love me best?" Insights into where the trials and trails of life might lead became clear by tests most potent on Halloween night.

Postcard marked B.W. 374, printed in Germany. Mailed Bradford, Pennsylvania, October 30, 1909.

• Mix grated nutmeg, hazelnut, and walnut meats with butter and sugar to form small "pills" to be eaten at bedtime. If pleasant dreams follow, a gentleman will be your lot. Dreams of difficulties foreshadow marriage to a laborer; those of bad storms or great disturbances presage marriage to a ne'er-do-well.

• Dust the top of your nightstand with corn meal on Halloween night. Ghosts will appear later to trace the name of your future mate as you sleep.

• Bake a ring and a key into a loaf cake. Whomever is served the slice containing the ring will marry in the near future. The diner who gets the key is fated to take a journey.

Vintage Halloween postcard. Mailed Toledo, Ohio, October 30, 1908.

THE LUCKY CAKE

A cake that's full of charms can be made on
Hallowe'en
And it causes lots of fun as is very quickly seen.
Choose one that's quick to bake, made of any
simple batter,
Let each girl help blend and stir in a merry din
and chatter.
Trinkets wrapped in papers oiled must be stirred in at
the very last,
And whoever cuts one out, will her future find
forecast.
She who finds the wedding ring will soon be a
happy wife,
She who finds the wheel will wander far and wide
throughout her life.
She who cuts the dime, cuts wealth, and the key
unlocks all hearts,
But the thimble means the spinster from whom
romance swift departs.
For the others naught is stated, but at least they have
a treat
In a cake they have constructed that is very good
to eat.

The Jolly Hallowe'en Book, *1937*

• Write the names of your love interests on small pieces of paper. Roll the papers into individual bits of a dough made from flour and water, and then place them all into a tub of water. The first name to rise up will be that of your future mate.

• Directly before going to bed, eat a small "pill" made of butter, sugar, and nut meats. If you are fated to marry a rich man, your sleep will be filled with dreams of gold. Marriage to a tradesman is signaled by tumultuous reveries accompanied by odd noises. Thunder and lightning presage marriage to a traveler.

• Invite six guests to share a bowl of crowdie— a traditional Halloween treat of whipped sweet cream and spiced apple sauce—into which two rings, two marbles, and two coins have been mixed. Fortune-seekers must dip a spoonful of the concoction and taste it, being mindful not to swallow the charms. Those who find rings will soon marry. The coins are symbolic of wealth and the marbles foretell a cold single life. A spoonful of crowdie alone symbolizes a life of sweet uncertainty.

Above, right: Valentine & Sons Publishing Co. Ltd., Montreal and Toronto. Postally unused.

Raphael Tuck & Sons "Hallowe'en" Post Cards series, No. 150. Mailed Pittsburgh, Pennsylvania, October 30, 1908.

• Carefully break a raw egg into a small glass cup or bowl and interpret the shape it takes for clues about the future. A house shape, for example, suggests that a change of residence may be in store. A trunk shape suggests travel to faraway places and the form of a hat suggests news about a student soon to graduate. After the divinations have been read, the fates can be sealed by pouring the eggs into a common bowl for the host to prepare *almoundyn eyroun*, an omelet made with raisins, almonds, honey, and spices.

• Bake a cake containing a ring, a thimble, a penny, and a dime. Marriage within the year is fated for the one who cuts the slice containing the ring. The thimble foretells spinsterhood; the penny, widowhood; and the dime, a legacy or riches.

Vintage Halloween postcard marked No. 2097. Postally unused.

• Tightly pack a bowl with flour and insert a ring vertically into some part. When the bowl is full, invert it onto a plate and invite fortune-seekers to cut a thin slice from the mound using a sharp knife. The guest whose slice contains the ring will be the first to marry.

• Make a wish while drinking a cup of tea. Your fortune can be told from the tea leaves according to this rhyme:

One leaf alone, alone you'll be,
Two together, the altar you'll see;
Three in groups, your wish you'll gain,
Four, a letter from a loving swain;
Five, good news a letter will bring,
Six in a row, an engagement ring;
Seven together, great fortune awaits
For you, so say the Tea-cup Fates;
Bring you company, great and small;
Tea leaves many and dotted fine
Are of bad luck the surest sign;
Tea leaves few and clean the rim,
Your cup with joy o'erflows the brim.

Hallowe'en Hilarity, *1924*

Vintage Halloween postcard marked CS658. Postmark illegible.

Postcard marked B.W. 374, printed in Germany. Mailed Chester, Pennsylvania, October 29, 1909.

• Place a dozen kernels of popcorn in a wire popper and hold it over an open flame. The number of kernels that remain unpopped signify the number of years before marriage.

• Ask a family member to bring you a small piece of dry bread at bedtime. Without speaking, eat the bread slowly as you make a wish and think the most pleasant thoughts possible. If that night your dreams are sweet and peaceful, you are assured that your wish will come true.

• Dip a teaspoon in a bowl of rice and count off the kernels to the appropriate rhyme. The chants may be repeated if necessary, and the last kernel will point to the vocation of your future mate.

For Girls

Rich man, poor man
Policeman, plumber,
Merchant, doctor,
Lawyer, drummer,
Blacksmith, grocer,
Druggist, teacher,
Artist, dentist,
Banker, preacher.

For Boys

Rich girl, poor girl, suffragette;
Waitress, milliner, farmerette;
School ma'am, actress, stenographer,
Musician, trained nurse, dressmaker;
Bookkeeper, house maid, author, clerk,
Telephone girl, and a lazy shirk.

Hallowe'en Hilarity, *1924*

A Charm to Say on HALLOWEEN

Halloween's the very time
To get your wish by some old rhyme,
Say these words and think of me,
Luck will follow fast and free,
"Eenty - teenty - tibbity - fig
Luck come little — luck come big!"
Friends will flock and dreams come true
And great good fortune follow you.

Circa 1920s Halloween card favor.

THE BOWLS OF FATE

THE SPELL OF THE WATER

Three cups of water in a row—
One foul, one fair,
And one quite bare;
And then, blindfolded, up you go,
Dip your left hand, and it will show
Just what the fates prepare.
The fair one means a maid for wife,
The foul, a widow, pain and strife,
The bare, a bachelor for life.

Bright Ideas for Hallowe'en, *1920*

When spells were cast under the bewitching aura of Halloween night, even ordinary bowls assumed mystical proportions. By way of a charm alternately referred to as the "luggies" (so called after small bowls with handles shaped like the ancient Druidic lamps) or the "bowls (or saucers) of fate," a kaleidoscope of fortunes could be foreseen by making a random selection amongst bowls filled with tokens that represented what the future held in store.

One old Scottish version of "the three luggies" called for an empty bowl along with one each containing clear and cloudy water to be set out in front of the fireplace. Blindfolded guests were then invited to place their hands in one of the bowls. A choice of clean water presaged a mate young and fair, the cloudy water symbolized widowhood, and the empty bowl foreshadowed what was often euphemistically termed "a life of single blessedness."

Vintage Halloween postcard marked No. 2097. Mailed Baltimore, Maryland, October 30, 1909.

"Mirror Series" postcard marked No. 248F, LSC. Mailed Lakewood, Ohio, October 30, 1913.

More desirable fortunes awaited those asked to select from three bowls of colored water. Red water foretold great fortune; blue, a trip across water; and clear, a great honor to be bestowed. Regardless of how many "luggies" were employed or the nature of their contents, though, diligent hosts repositioned the bowls for each subsequent guest to ensure that Fate was not unduly influenced.

It's impossible to know for certain whether tradition, curiosity, or even the availability of suitable dinnerware determined how many bowls were filled, but many fanciful variations of this augury existed. The degree of ease or difficulty that lay ahead on the road of life, for example, might be determined by making a random selection amongst seven saucers. The dish that held a bit of dough ensured a life of ease, while one containing a tiny elephant charm foretold luck. The remaining tokens included a rubber band (symbolic of a lively or "snappy" life), a sharp thorn (representing a troublesome path), clear water (indicative of an unruffled life), and a key (symbolic of good luck). As was often the case, an empty bowl stood for bachelor- or spinsterhood.

Circa 1915 Halloween postcard.

In any instance, the eclectic destinies foretold by various versions of the "luggies" or saucers of fate traditionally focused on life's most significant milestones, and the following variations were all once prescribed to satisfy the curiosity of inquisitive partygoers.

• Group together four saucers and fill one each with clear water, soapy water, and pebbles; the fourth and final saucer should remain empty. The guest who chooses clear water will enjoy a happy marriage. Soapy water suggests widowhood; the pebbles, a life of toil; and the empty saucer, a life of single blessedness.

• Place three dishes in a row—one containing a ring, the second, water, and the third, a clump of dirt. Ask fortune-seekers to spin around three times and then, without looking, touch one of the dishes. Those selecting the dish with the ring will marry soon, while those choosing the one with water will not marry at all. The dish filled with dirt is symbolic of a speedy death.

• Blindfold guests and ask them to place their hands in one of four saucers. The saucer containing dirt represents divorce. That of water foretells an ocean trip. The dish containing a ring symbolizes marriages, and the one holding a rag foreshadows spinster- or bachelorhood.

Postcard marked series 339E. Postmark removed with stamp.

H. B. Griggs artist-signed postcard marked L.& E. series 2262. Postally unused.

PURE, FOUL, OR EMPTY

Three little dishes, all in a row,
One holds clear water, that well I know;
One holds foul water, one none at all.
Blindfold I seek them. Which will me call?
If the clear water, happy I'll wed.
If the foul water, unhappy instead.
If the sad, empty, ah, woe, woe is me!
A lonely old (spinster/bachelor) forever I'll be.

The Jolly Hallowe'en Book, *1937*

• Ask guests to wear blindfolds and select one of three saucers. The vessel filled with clear water foretells a charming, youthful mate; the saucer with soapy water presages life as a widow or widower. Those selecting the empty saucer are fated to remain unwed.

• Direct blindfolded guests to place their hands upon one of four bowls. Choosing a bowl filled with water symbolizes a peaceful, happy life. A bowl of wine signifies a rich and noble career. A bowl of vinegar foretells widowhood while an empty bowl foreshadows bachelor- or spinsterhood.

• Ask a blindfolded guest to select from three bowls of fate: if she finds moss, luxury is in her future. Dust symbolizes an auto trip; thorns portend an unhappy marriage.

Halloween postcard marked H17 CN.
Mailed New Hampshire, October 30, 1913.

• To discover your fortune, don a blindfold and choose from these seven bowls of fate:

Red cloth—you'll have a happy marriage
Blue cloth—follow the sea
A thorn—you'll be unlucky in romance
A forked stick—marry a widow or widower
Clean water—a life of single blessedness
A double knot—marriage is at hand
Moss—you'll live a life of luxury

• Arrange seven bowls in front of the fireplace and ask blindfolded guests to seek their fate by choosing amongst them. A bowl of moss symbolizes a life of ease, one containing white hairs represents long life, and a branch of thorns foretells many troubles. The bowl of soil represents travel. That containing a double knot symbolizes a speedy marriage; a forked twig, marriage to a widow or widower. Clear water symbolized single blessedness.

Circa 1950 heavy cardboard horn.

Halloween postcard marked H17 CN. Postally unused.

Halloween postcard marked H17 CN. Mailed Scranton, Pennsylvania, October 28, 1914.

HALLOWE'EN

Wi' merry sangs an' friendly
cracks,
I wat they did na weary;
And unco tales, an' funnie
jokes —
Their sports were cheap an'
cheery.

BURNS — "Hallowe'en"

Circa 1920 illustration from children's magazine.

Opposite, lead-in: *Circa 1940s papier-mâché lantern with tissue paper facial inserts and candle holder at base. The lantern measures 5fl" high and has identical faces on both sides.*

Circa 1900 magazine illustration.

THE LEGEND OF THE JACK O'LANTERN

For many the round and jolly jack o'lanterns that light brisk October nights with grins of equal merriment and menace are the quintessential Halloween icon. According to Irish legend, the "Jack" after whom these earthy homemade lanterns were named was a miserly and unpleasant gent unable to enter heaven because of uncharitable deeds in life and unwelcome in the netherworld because of a trick he had played on the devil. With no where else to go when he died, Jack was doomed to roam the earth until Judgment Day, his path guided by a hollow turnip illuminated by a single coal from hell.

For centuries, quaint lanterns carved from turnips or beets were commonly used in Scotland and Ireland to light the paths of travelers crossing the countryside. Makers of the lanterns embellished their creations with grotesque facial features to frighten away ghostly spirits who walked the earth on Halloween night.

When immigrants from the British Isles moved to America, they soon discovered that pumpkins were ideally suited for use as their traditional carved vegetable beacons. Pumpkins and jack o'lanterns have shared a festive bond ever since.

Top: *Circa 1920s heavy cardboard dessert "pick" decoration with fortune on back by Dennison Manufacturing.*

Right: *Circa 1920 Halloween party invitaion.*

Postcard marked B.W. 374, printed in Germany. Mailed Milwaukee, Wisconsin, October 31, 1910.

Postcard marked B.W. 374, printed in Germany. Mailed Cincinnati, Ohio, November 1, 1909.

A CORNUCOPIA OF CHARMS

May Jack-o-lanterns burning bright
Of soft and golden hue
Pierce through the future's veil and show
What fate now holds for you.

By goblins of the cornfield stark
By witches dancing on the green
By pumpkins grinning in the dark
I wish you luck this Hallowe'en.

Verse from old Halloween postcards

Under the silent but certain watch of hobgoblins and ghosts, will o' the wisps and bogies, old-fashioned Halloween fortune-telling rituals took a beguiling variety of twists and turns as the fates were coaxed to reveal secrets of love, matrimony, friendship, or riches. The night was ripe for augury, and early-twentieth-century partygoers were advised by popular periodicals and party guides alike to gather by the mellow flicker of grinning jack o'lanterns to practice these novel charms:

By Needles and Pins

• Ask those gathered to sit on round bottles laid lengthwise on the floor and try to thread a needle. The first to succeed will be the first to marry.

• Set twenty-five new needles on a plate and pour water over them. Those that cross denote enemies.

• Mark greased needles for partygoers and float them in a large basin of water. The needles will be affected by the attraction of gravitation (or perhaps the spirits of Halloween?) and the manner in which a person's needle behaves towards another is deemed prophetic.

Circa 1910 Halloween postcard. Postally unused.

NEEDLE PROPHETS

Take twenty-five new needles
And lay them on a plate,
Pour water gently o'er them
Then you may read your fate;
For those that cross mean enemies,
And you may well beware.
Their tongues are keen and quick to pierce
Like all those needles there.

The Jolly Hallowe'en Book, *1937*

H. B. Griggs artist-signed postcard marked L.& E. series 2262. Mailed Mattoon, Illinois, October 30, 1910.

Old Yarns

Out I throw this ball of yarn,
My own true love's sweet name to learn;
I wind it in until 'tis held,
And then the winds his name will tell.

Hallowe'en Pranks and Parties, *1927*

- Toss a ball of yarn from an upstairs window. By chanting "I wind, who hauds (holds)?" a reflection of your intended will appear in the window or his name will be heard whispered aloud. If a prayer is repeated backwards as the yarn is wound, the fates will reveal a fortune.

Cast a ball of yarn in a darksome place,
Wind till the thread is caught
Then cry "Who holds?" and a voice will speak
His name who shall share your lot.

Verse on old Halloween postcard

Match Tests

• Light a match over a sink filled with water and hold it until it is completely burned out. The direction in which the tip falls off tells the direction in which your true love can be found. If the match burns up without breaking, your true love is present and you may have one wish.

To blow out a flame, through a funnel of paper,
Is really a most informational caper.
If you blow it the first time you'll marry for love.
If the second, because you rate beauty above:
If the third, you will marry for money in sight,
And if not then, your marriage will just be for spite.
The Jolly Hallowe'en Book, *1937*

• Take a lighted match in your right hand and use it to trace a complete circle in the air. If the match is still burning when the motion is complete, you are certain to marry within the year. The match can then be safely extinguished.

Halloween postcard marked H17 CN.
Mailed Worcester, Massachusetts, October 30, 1913.

Ringing the Chimes

A wedding ring is hung up in a doorway,
This wedding ring is hung up by a string;
Just twelve feet back there stands a lovely maiden
Who points a pencil at the hung up ring.
With cautious step she moves on toward the doorway
She dare not let the pencil rise or fall,
She aims to slip it first straight through the trinket
For then she soon will hear Dan Cupid's call.
The Jolly Hallowe'en Book, *1937*

• Tie a wedding ring to a silk thread and suspend it inside a goblet. Repeat the alphabet slowly and when the ring moves to strike the glass, take note of the letter being spoken. Begin the alphabet once again and in this way you will spell the name or initials of your future mate.

Halloween postcard marked L.& E. series 2231.
Mailed Kansas City, Missouri, October 28, 1909.

Fate of the Ashes

• Blow with force into a handful of fine ashes. If they fly back over your face, your future husband will be a tyrant; if they do not, then happiness is assured.

Salt Sense

THE SALT AND WATER RACE

This is a stern test, maidens,
But it will tell your fate;
Fill your mouths with water,
Let the hour be late.
Fill right hands with salt,
Make them tightly lock;
Then at given signal
Run around the block.
Woe to her who giggles—
Salt or water loses,
But hail the first name listened to—
'Twill be the mate she chooses.

The Jolly Hallowe'en Book, *1937*

• Take three doses of salt two minutes apart. Go to bed backwards, lie on your right side, and do not move until morning. This charm will cause dreams that foretell important events.

• One old test of fate called for young ladies to take a mouthful of salt and go to the cellar carrying a mirror in one hand and a glass of water or lighted candle in the other. As they tried not to swallow the salt, they were to gaze into the mirror as they repeated this chant:

Looking glass, I hope to see
The one who is my destiny!
Ask him now to give a sign
That some day he will be all mine.

Vintage postcard marked series No. 363, Hallowe'en 6 designs. Postally unused.

Apparel Auguries

• Secretly tally the buttons on the coat of the first person you meet of the opposite sex according to this chant:

> *He (or she) loves me; he loves me ever;*
> *He comes soon; he comes never;*
> *He goes far; he stays near;*
> *Proposes (or says "yes") this year.*
>
> Hallowe'en Happenings, *1921*

• Take an old shoe and ask guests to toss it over their shoulders. The direction in which the footwear points shows the direction that individual will soon travel. It is considered very unlucky for the shoe to fall with its sole facing up.

• Hang a wet sheet in front of the fire on Halloween to see a vision of your future mate.

• Place a lighted candle in the sink. Hold a thread over the flame and begin to count slowly. The number counted before the thread burns in two denotes the number of years before you will marry.

Raphael Tuck & Sons "Hallowe'en" Post Cards, series No. 150. Postally unused.

Pleasant Reflections

• Go to a spring of water carrying a lamp and peer into the depths; a reflection of your future mate will appear. If you are reluctant to go out after dark, approach the same spring in daylight hours while carrying a broken egg in a glass. Pour some of the spring water into the glass and you will see images of both the man you will marry and the children you will have together.

Raphael Tuck & Sons "Hallowe'en" Post Cards, series No. 150. Postally unused.

Postcard marked Halloween series 303. Mailed Chicago, Illinios, October 30, 1911.

MANY SHAPES OF THINGS TO COME

THE MAGIC LEAD

Melted lead poured out in water
Strange shapes will assume,
So if you'll these forms decipher
You may well presume
That they represent your future,
Plain as plain can be.
For example, ships will tell you
That you'll go to sea.
Books will point you out a scholar,
Guns, a soldier, brave and bold.
Everyone shows something different,
Waiting to be read and told.

The Jolly Hallowe'en Book, *1937*

The pairing of lead with water represented a peculiar means indeed of divining the future. Auguries performed with these ingredients called upon fortune seekers to put a small piece of lead in a spoon and melt it over an open flame. The liquefied metal would then be poured into a container of water or sand, and the shape it assumed after it had cooled could be studied for clues regarding the occupational calling of self or that of a future mate.

A book shape was said to indicate a scribbler or an editor; if a coin formed, then riches were assured. A pill shape denoted a doctor; a parchment, a lawyer; a three-cornered plow shape, a farmer. If no significance could be discerned from the shape the drop assumed, a life of loneliness was foreshadowed.

Postcard marked Halloween series No. 1, 1072. Mailed Baltimore, Maryland, October 23, 1908.

A variation of this augury called for interpreting the shapes formed when a tiny bit of melted lead was poured through a wedding ring or key into a dish of water. Drops resembling bells foretold a wedding within the year; a torch or lamp image denoted fame; a pen or ink bottle represented an author as a future companion; a horn of plenty presaged wealth; a bag or trunk foretold travel.

Another test called for melted lead to be dropped into a bowl of cool water through the handle opening of a key (imagine the "skeleton keys" of yesteryear that boasted large open notches at the top) and the shape it formed interpreted according to these truths: a single round drop foretold spinsterhood; several round scattered drops foreshadowed a journey over land; irregular-shaped drops foretold many affairs of the heart; and one long, lumpy mass symbolized a life filled with troubles. It was also believed that melted lead poured into the sand would cool to form the shape of one's future mate's first initial.

Party guides also advised generations past that they might substitute the more readily managed yet equally authentic elements of melted wax (dropped into cool water) or egg whites (dropped into boiling water) in lieu of handling lead. In any instance, those who challenged fate by these quaint rituals needed to lend ample applications of imagination to interpret their results.

Top: *Vintage Halloween postcard marked series 339F. Mailed Montreal, P.Q., October 31, 1924.*

Middle: *Postcard marked series 339A. Mailed Salem, Oregon, October 22, 1913.*

Bottom: *Halloween postcard marked series 339D. Mailed Plymouth, New Hampshire, October 21, 1919.*

FATE'S REFLECTIONS

Halloween postcard marked series 216B, LSC.
Mailed Springfield, Ohio, October 30, 1912.

With Hallowe'en candles burning bright
Beneath the moon's bewitching light
May ghosts and goblins grant to you
That all your wishes shall come true.

Verse on old Halloween postcard

Seasoned soothsayers have traditionally used crystal balls to explore the paths the future might take. Inquisitive novices, guided by a combination of curiosity and old-fashioned beliefs, turned to mirrors for telling, if fleeting, glimpses of their loves most true.

One Halloween augury promised smitten romantics a clear reflection of their sweethearts if they carried a mirror and repeated this rhyme as they walked backward in the moonlight:

Round and round, O stars so fair!
Ye travel and search out everywhere;
I pray you, sweet stars, now show to me
This night who my future mate shall be.
(If in the mirror your lover is seen,
You'll surely be happy on Hallowe'en!)

Games for Hallowe'en, *1912*

Halloween postcard marked series 80F.
Postally unused.

Halloween postcard marked series 63A.
Postmarked October 30, 1918.

Halloween postcard marked No. 6500. Mailed Indiana Harbor, Indiana, September 23, 1919.

This same chant could be repeated indoors by substituting a hand-held candle for the glow of the moon. Party planning guides also counseled inquirers to hazard a walk downstairs backward, holding a candle above their heads. Upon reaching the bottom, they could turn suddenly and find themselves standing astride the ones they wished for.

Now to see your lover tried and true,
I advise you this to do:
Take a mirror new and bright
In your left hand at Twelve to night
and a lighted candle in your right.

Rhyme from old Halloween postcard

Vintage Halloween postcard. Postally unused.

A further charm called for participants to cautiously descend the cellar steps backwards with a candle in one hand, a mirror in the other, and a mouthful of salt. At the foot of the steps they would see their future mates gazing over their shoulders into the mirrors. A simpler ritual called for the lovelorn to eat an apple in front of a mirror on Halloween to see an image of their intended asking for the last bite.

Let this design on you prevail
To try this trick (it cannot fail)
Back down the stairs with candle dim
And in the mirror you'll see HIM!

Rhyme from old Halloween postcard

"Mirror Series" postcard No. 248B, marked LSC. Postally unused.

Circa 1920 Halloween postcard.

P. F. Volland & Co., Chicago, No. 4043. Dated October 30, 1913.

Hallowe'en

By JOHN VANCE CHENEY

SHE ate the apple—as did Eve—
And looked into the glass;
She said, "The Fates will not deceive
A little lonely lass."

SHE ate the apple, rind and all,
So that the Fates could see,
Although she was so lone and small,
She trusted utterly.

THE Fates—not always wholly kind,—
Now said among themselves,—
"Here is a darling to our mind;
Send for the happy elves!"

THE happy elves came trooping in,
Ready to run or fly;
And when she did the charm begin,
They all were standing by.

SHE held the candle up; the flame
Went flickering to and fro:
The happy elves wrote out *his* name,
And drew *his* face below.

SHE kissed the mirror (yes she did;
And I know what she said;
But I wont tell it—heaven forbid!)
And then she went to bed.

Illustrated poem entitled "Hallowe'en" from the October 1906 issue of The Delineator *magazine.*

CANDLELIGHT CAPERS

With Hallowe'en candles burning bright
Beneath the moon's bewitching light
May ghosts & goblins grant to you
That all your wishes shall come true.

Verse on early twentieth-century postcard

More than anything else, light enables us to see and interpret things more clearly. As the abbreviated days of autumn readied the stage for the arrival of darker hours that would soon be escorted by the coming of winter, the telling glow of candlelight played a prominent role in Halloweens past. Flames from candles and bonfires alike were believed to welcome good spirits and prevent evil ones from coming near. "A Nut-Crack Night Party," a fanciful tale about Halloween fortunetelling that appeared in the November 1907 issue of *Harper's Bazaar*, emphasized the importance of bonfires.

> "'We are all to go first to the bonfire,' she explained to them. 'None of our efforts to peer into the future can avail until the bad spirits who abound tonight have been consumed.'"

In ancient times, the light of coals carried in hollowed-out turnips lit paths through the haunting countryside, and hosts of early-twentieth-century Halloween revels were admonished to ensure that departing guests were guided by lantern's glow. "Guests must not be allowed to leave without a protecting light," organizers of Halloween events were advised by *The Delineator* magazine back in 1919, "for who can tell what would happen on Hallowe'en? So, as the couples start for home, provide them with tiny lighted lanterns, (either) jack-o'-lanterns made of papier-mache, or weird Japanese lanterns."

Raphael Tuck & Sons "Hallowe'en" Post Cards, series No. 197.
Mailed Chelsea, Massachusetts, October 28, 1914.

The glow of candles on Halloween illuminated the future for intrepid romantics with a host of charms as bright as their flames. One old ritual said to have produced many a heart-stopping moment for ladies attired in traditional trailing gowns required partygoers to boldly jump over a dozen candles. The number left burning afterward would represent the number of months, or years, before marriage.

Alternatively, candles designated to represent the months of the year were lined up on the floor with ample space between them. Fortune-seekers then leapt over the lighted tapers one by one, the month of their marriage presaged by the candle that was extinguished first.

Another old-fashioned divination called upon revelers to jump over a single lighted candle set in the middle of the floor. Those who managed to clear the candle without disturbing it were guaranteed a year free of trouble or anxiety. Unfortunate souls who knocked over the candle were fated to twelve months of woe starting, perhaps, with a raging fire in the living room.

Circa 1915 Halloween postcard.

Halloween series No. 27. Mailed Denver, Colorado, October 30, 1920.

Candle colors also took on significance in Halloween prophecies. One such divination called for half a dozen candles—one each of red, yellow, pink, white, green, and blue—to be grouped atop a table. Standing at a predetermined distance, fortune-seekers were asked to blow toward the candles three times; the personal qualities of their future mates, be they wealthy scholars or industrious ladies' men, were said to be revealed by the candles that had been extinguished:

Candle of red denotes that you
Will win a spouse constant and true;
White denotes whate'er his station
Your mate will have a fine reputation;
'Tis foretold by candle of yellow
He'll be a very industrious fellow;
By candle pink you are told
That he'll be handsome to behold;
And always, so candle of green doth tell,
He will provide for you amply and well;
While blue proclaims with sure discerning,
That he will be a man of learning.

Hallowe'en Hilarity, *1924*

Still other candlelight soothsaying customs like these tempted Halloween partygoers of yesteryear with glimmers of what the future held.

• Lead a blindfolded guest to a table set with three lighted candles. Guide her in taking six steps away from the candles, then six steps in return, when she should then blow in the direction of the candles. If the first candle is extinguished, she will marry within a year; the second candle, two years; the third, three years. If no candles are blown out, the inquirer will remain unwed.

Vintage Halloween postcard mailed Allentown, Pennsylvania, October 28 (no year given).

There are twelve candles in a row—
Jump them, maidens fair!
Each one is named for a month, you know.
If the draught blows out one flickering flame,
When you jump it, maidens fair;
So jump them, maidens fair!

The Jolly Hallowe'en Book, *1937*

• Place seven lighted candles on a tabletop. Ask the fortune-seeker to don a blindfold, turn around three times, and then blow three times in the direction of the candles; the number left burning represents the number of years before marriage. If all of the candles remain lighted, a wedding will take place within the year. If all are extinguished, however, the inquirer will not marry.

• Place twelve lighted candles in a row. Lead the fortune-seeker to the candles, and then ask her to turn around three times and blow once toward them. Whichever candle is blown out represents the month in which her wedding will take place. If no candles are extinguished, she will live her life in single blessedness.

• Light a large tallow candle in the center of a table. Stand at a distance of three paces and take three tries to blow out the flame as this chant is repeated:

Wed a rich man's son if blown out in one
A man of rank if blown out in two,
A workman if blown out in three,
But fail on three, unwed you shall be.

Above: *Halloween postcard. Mailed Akron, Ohio, October 23, 1916.*

Left: *H. B. Griggs artist-signed postcard, L. & E. series 2262. Mailed Fort Collins, Colorado, October 28, 1912.*

• Arrange four candles on a table. The number of puffs taken to blow out a candle foretells the number of years before marriage. The color of the candle extinguished first takes on significance according to this rhyme:

If the candle be of white,
It most surely spells delight.
They who choose a candle red,
Will forever be well fed.
Candle green marks jealousy,
So beware or sad you'll be.
Let me see—a candle yellow,
Shows for mate a right good fellow.

Dennison's Bogie Book, *1921*

Whitney Made, Worcester, Massachusetts. Postmarked Pekin, Illinois, October 30 (year illegible).

Whitney Made, Worcester, Massachusetts. Postally used, information illegible.

H. B. Griggs artist-signed postcard No. 2214. Mailed Washington, D.C., October 31 (year illegible).

The message on the back of this 1911 postcard includes some homemade illustrations.

VERY TRULY YOURS

From a hasty scrawl to regal-looking script, the messages penned on the backs of illustrated vintage postcards offer a peek at life during the early 1900s. Inexpensive both to buy and to mail, the old postcards delivered news, well wishes, holiday salutations, and, for especially lucky recipients, even gossip, all with a colorful flair. Getting a postcard from a friend or loved one doubtless added something special to an ordinary day, and whether sentimental recipients cherished the written greeting, its eye-catching messenger, or both, they saw fit to carefully tuck the colorful missives away in attics, bureaus, books, or drawers where they awaited discovery by a generation of admiring collectors. Revisit early-twentieth-century America by these messages found on the correspondence sections of Halloween postcards from the medium's "Golden Age."

Miss Ida Davis/Loveland, Ohio, November 1, 1909

My Dear little niece;

How are you these lovely Autumn days? I wish I could be with you gathering nuts, pumpkins. Tell Papa I received his card and will write him soon. With love to Papa, Mama and Grandma.

Aunt Mae

Miss Minnie Palmer/Pittsfield, New Hampshire, October 26, 1917

I hope you will enjoy Halloween. I am at Center Strafford for the winter. Are you still Freezing in Pittsfield? With love.

Ella

Mrs. A. Williamson/Pasadena, California,
October 30, 1914

Dear Aunt,

I send you A lot of kisses and low to look out that witch don't get you out their. I saw her downtown yesterday.

From Mildred

Miss I. Louisa Beam/Wadsworth, Ohio, October 31, 1908

Dear Little Louisa,

Pops shipped your apples Thursday. We were in (illegible) yesterday and saw Mr. & Mrs. Bryan and their special train. Heard most of his speech. Do not get into mischief tonight.

Aunt Mary Louise

Postcard marked series No. 298 Hallowe'en, 6 designs. Postmark illegible.

Miss Marie Cooper/Interlaken, Massachusetts,
October 29, 1909

My dear Marie:—

How are you all I wonder. You are as busy as a bee at school, I suppose. Doesn't the country look just beautiful! Kind remembrances to all with much love to little Marie.

F. Bodden

Miss Florence Johnson/Long Island, New York,
October 31, 1910

Dear Florence,

I will now wish you a jolly Halloween and my face is better but it ain't healed yet.

Little Fred

Dr. Stanley Hill/Effingham, Illinois, October 30, 1911

How do you do, Doc! Received your card. Oh, this is a great old place. Something doing all the time. Had a Hallowe'en celebration last eve and am going to another Tues. If there are no Hallowe'en stunts then it is "parlor games." Ahem! Better come to Peoria.

E.

Master Glenn Dale Caswell/Knoxville, Iowa,
October 30, 1920

Dear Glenn Dale:—

How are you? Did you take Brownie to town with you? I rec'd your mamma's letter today, & will answer soon. I am still loafing.

Grayce

Miss Gertrude Wyman/Louisville, Kentucky,
October 29, 1909

Hope the peeling will form the right initial.

Sincerely, Lula Alles

Mr. Samuel Moore/Derry, Pennsylvania, October 29, 1912

Hello Kiddo:—

I just sent Ivan a card warning him not to steal too many gates. I know you do not do such stunts so I shall not warn you.

J.L.

Mr. William Cyrus Simmons, October 31, 1917

William have you got a Pumpkin with a face cut in it for Halloween. See how this little boys pumpkin scares the little girl.

Grandma

Raphael Tuck & Sons "Hallowe'en" series of Post Cards, No. 190. Mailed St. Louis, Missouri, October 30, 1914.

Vintage Halloween postcard. Postally unused.

Halloween postcard marked series 1239C. Mailed Randolph, New York, October 21, 1926.

Halloween postcard marked series 1239B. Postally unused.

Mr. Buford Davis/Indianapolis, Indiana, October 30, 1918

Dear Buford,

Are you all keeping well or is everybody having Flu out there? This is the third week our school has been closed. Wish you were here to help make my jack o lantern.

Miriam

Marie Gurney/Akron, Ohio, October 23, 1916

Hello Marie got a pumpkin face made yet I've got one for paul paul's papa feel bad again had the doctor friday. Those skirts mama made were dandy. Good Bye

Aunt Pearl

German-made die-cut of cat and moon made of heavily-embossed cardboard.

A toast to Hallowe'en!
It comes but once a year,
But it brings joys a-plenty
The one night that it's here.
Here's to you, my friends,
May success be yours today;
May propitious fates attend you,
And good luck with you stay.
May charms and divinations
Show future joys and blisses,
With love to keep you happy,
Love flavored with sweet kisses!
Here's a toast to Hallowe'en,
And may its revels last!

Hallowe'en Merrymakers, *1930*

Halloween postcard marked No. 581-4. Postally unused.

RESOURCE GUIDE

Vintage Halloween postcards date from the period between 1900 and approximately 1927; cards and other photography by the author.

Vintage Halloween ephemera photographed by the author appears with the consent of The Beistle Company, Shippensburg, PA, and Avery Dennison, Pasadena, CA.

October 31, 1912 THE YOUTH'S COMPANION FOR ALL THE FAMILY 601

CHILDREN'S PAGE

ON HALLOWE'EN NIGHT

BY NANCY BYRD TURNER

DRAWINGS BY SEARS GALLAGHER

Suppose this year at Hallowe'en, without a bit of warning,
The roly-poly pumpkin heads we cut and carved that morning
Should grow them bodies, legs and feet,
And quick, from post and steeple,
Come skipping 'mongst us pert and fleet,
Real, frisky pumpkin people!
Suppose that you and I had just completed one that minute,
As day grew late, down by the gate, and set a candle in it,
So that its eyes were deep and wide,
Its mouth a grinning yellow,
Then turn to find him at our side,
A living pumpkin fellow?
Suppose we ran with twinkling heels and met a throng advancing,
Their teeth a-row, their eyes aglow, all whirling, pranking, prancing;
Suppose they twirled us merrily,
The whole dark landscape lighting—
This Hallowe'en, I think, would be
A little too exciting!

BILLY POPGUN AND THE FIELD MOUSE

BY MILO WINTER

BILLY had begun to feel chilly during his meeting with the Frogs, and his sympathy had already been given to the Field Mice. He was not cold-blooded, like a Frog, and a warm little house would be cozy.

At last the Mouse stopped in front of a bunch

Although the outside of the house was not pretty to look at, the inside was as snug and warm and neat as it could be. It was a great deal better than the cold Marsh, and Billy decided without any further hesitation that the Field Mice were quite right in building houses. The Frogs could never know how comfort-

He followed the Mouse down out of the house, to where a short distance away there was a great ear of corn that looked as big as a log to Billy. The Mouse broke off a kernel, gave it to Billy, and took another for himself.

Suddenly he noticed that the Mouse was no longer talking to him, but to some one behind a piece of corn husk. He peeped round, and there was the Grasshopper that he had seen when he first started out.

"This is probably the very field," Billy

squeak, if he would please tell the Frogs what he thought about the houses. But the Frogs never found out what Billy thought. He did not stop for anything after that till he reached his home. And so now, whenever you happen to be near a Marsh at night, you can hear them still arguing the old question. As for the Field Mice, they continue to build their houses. But you will never be invited in to see how cozy it is inside.

"On Hallowe'en Night" from The Youth's Companion, *October 31, 1912.*

Books and Periodicals

"A Hallowe'en German," *The Delineator*, October 1894.

"A Jolly Good Time for Hallowe'en," *The Delineator,* October 1909.

Ainslee, Margaret. "Hints for Hallowe'en Hilarities," *The Ladies' Home Journal*, October 1910.

Alverson, Lilian and others. *Novelty Hallowe'en Collection for Children.* Franklin, Ohio: Eldridge Publishing Company, 1937.

Aspinwall, Marguerite. "A Hallowe'en Maypole," *Woman's Home Companion*, October 1925.

Bickford, Nana French. "A Hallowe'en Masquerade," *The Modern Priscilla*, October 1912.

Blain, Mary E. *Games for Hallowe'en*. New York: Barse & Hopkins Publishers, 1912.

Cosman, Madeleine Pelner. *Medieval Holidays and Festivals*. Charles Scribner's Sons, 1981.

Dennison Manufacturing Co. Dennison's *Bogie Book*. Framingham, Massachusetts: 1913, 1915, 1920, 1922, 1923, 1924, 1925, and 1926 editions; *Party Magazine*, October/November 1927; *Hallowe'en Parties: Decorations, Favors, Games and Stunts*, 1935.

Denton, Clara J. *Creepy Hallowe'en Celebrations*. Dayton, Ohio: Paine Publishing Company, 1926.

Dolan, Lenore K. *Handy Helps for Hallowe'en*. Franklin, Ohio: Eldridge Publishing Company, 1932.

Fales, Winnifred. "The Hallowe'en Party," *The Ladies' Home Journal*, October 1914.

"Fun for Hallowe'en," *The Ladies' Home Journal*, October 1907.

Guptill, Elizabeth F., Smith, Laura Rountree, and others. *Bright Ideas for Hallowe'en*. Lebanon, Ohio: March Brothers, 1920.

__________. *The Complete Hallowe'en Book*. Lebanon, Ohio: March Brothers, 1915.

"Hallowe'en Fun at Goblintown on the Spookville Road," *The Ladies' Home Journal*, October 1916.

"Hallowe'en Merrymakings," *The Ladies' Home Journal*, October 1909.

"The Hallowe'en Party," *The Ladies' Home Journal*, October 1913.

Hasbrook, Bertha. "A Nut-Crack Night Party," *Harper's Bazaar*, November 1907.

Heath, Catherine. "Hallowe'en Tricks and Fortunes," *The Delineator*, October 1911.

Hetrick, Lenore. *The Giant Hallowe'en Book*. Dayton, Ohio: Paine Publishing Company, 1934.

Hunt, Virginia. "What Kind of Party Can I Give?", *The Ladies' Home Journal*, October 1912.

Irish, Marie. *Hallowe'en Fun*. Syracuse, New York: The Willis N. Bugbee Company, 1927.

__________. *Hallowe'en Hilarity*. Dayton, Ohio: Paine Publishing Co., 1924.

__________. *Hallowe'en Merrymakers*. Syracuse, New York: The Willis N. Bugbee Company, 1930.

Circa 1915 Halloween postcard.

Irish, Marie. *Kiddies' Hallowe'en Book*. Syracuse, New York: The Willis N. Bugbee Co., 1931.

__________. *Spooky Hallowe'en Entertainments*. Dayton, Ohio: Paine Publishing Co., 1923.

Kenney, Helen. "Hallowe'en Favors," *Harper's Bazaar,* November 1911.

Kingsland, Mrs. Burton. "A Jolly Hallowe'en Party," *The Ladies' Home Journal*, October 1902.

Lloyd, Gladys. *Hallowe'en Pranks and Parties. Franklin, Ohio: Eldridge Entertainment House, 1927.*

__________. The Tip-Top Hallowe'en Book. Syracuse, New York: The Willis N. Bugbee Co., circa 1930.

March, Marjorie. "Entertaining Our Friends," *The Housekeeper*, October 1909.

Moore, Rebecca Deming. "Let's Have a Jack-o'-Lantern Frolic," *Woman's World*, October 1921.

Moran, Marie Eulalie. "Hallowe'en Fun," *The Ladies' Home Journal*, October 1906.

Morton, Frank. "A Kaleidoscope of Kales," *National Gardening*, September/October 1998.

1920 "Johnny Pumpkin Head" cardboard stand-up character by The Beistle Company, Shippensburg, Pennslyvania.

Cover of Halloween Frolic, *a booklet of music for "parlor and school entertainments" published by David C. Cook Publishing Co., Elgin, Illinois, 1908.*

Nicholson, Susan Brown. "Hallowe'en Customs on Post Cards," *Collectors' Showcase*, September/October 1984.

Norton, Jeannette Young. "A Hallowe'en Supper," *Good Housekeeping*, October 1911.

Parker, Marion Jane. *The Children's Party Book*. Chicago: Rogers & Company, 1924.

Preston, Effa E. *Hallowe'en Celebrations*. Dayton, Ohio: Paine Publishing Co., 1925.

"Quaint Hallowe'en Customs Well Worth Reviving," *Harper's Bazaar* November 1912.

Robinson, Elizabeth. "A Novel Hallowe'en Party," *Harper's Bazaar*, November 1904.

Rosenstein, Mark. *In Praise of Apples*. Asheville, North Carolina: Lark Books, 1996.

Rosiere, Gabrielle. "A Hallowe'en Party," *Woman's Home Companion*, October 1913.

Sackett, Ruth Virginia. "Entertainments for Hallowe'en: An Autumn-Leaf Jollification," *The Delineator*, October 1904.

Schauffler, Robert Haven. *Hallowe'en*. New York: Dodd, Mead and Company, 1958.

Sears, Anna Wentworth. "Games for Hallowe'en," *Harper's Bazaar*, October 1900.

Shipman, Dorothy and others. *The Jolly Hallowe'en Book*. Syracuse, New York: The Willis N. Bugbee Co., 1937.

Spicer, Dorothy Gladys. "Charms and Chants for Nutcrack Night," *American Home*, November 1933.

Staley, Cornelia. *Children's Party Book*. Decatur, Illinois: A. E. Staley Mfg. Co., 1935.

Sykora, Laura Gates. "Hallowe'en Merriment," *The Delineator*, October 1919.

Telford, Mae McGuire. "What Shall We Do For Hallowe'en?" *The Ladies' Home Journal*, October 1920.

Trappe, Ruth E. and McGehee, Ruth E. *Hallowe'en: Suggestions for Parties and Entertainments*. (c) Frederick M. Kerby, 1923.

"Two Jolly Hallowe'en Affairs," *Woman's Home Companion*, October 1912.

Van Derveer, Lettie C. *Hallowe'en Happenings*. Boston: Walter H. Baker Company, 1921.

Walsh, William S. *Curiosities of Popular Customs*. J.B. Lippincott Company, 1897.

Weeks, Grace L. "Merry Hallowe'en Larks," *The Ladies' Home Journal*, October 1903.

Yale, Elsie Duncan. "Halloween Round-up," *Woman's Home Companion*, October 1934.

Circa 1919 Halloween postcard.